The Rosary

WITH BISHOP ROBERT BARRON

Word on Fire, Park Ridge, IL 60068
© 2021 by Word on Fire Catholic Ministries
All rights reserved.

ISBN: 978-1-943243-73-0

Library of Congress Control Number: 2020924286
Barron, Robert, 1959–

Table of Contents

.... † ....

Introduction to the Rosary

. . . . † . . . .

Pope St. John Paul II

The Rosary of the Virgin Mary, which gradually took form in the second millennium under the guidance of the Spirit of God, is a prayer loved by countless Saints and encouraged by the Magisterium. Simple yet profound, it still remains, at the dawn of this third millennium, a prayer of great significance, destined to bring forth a harvest of holiness. It blends easily into the spiritual journey of the Christian life, which, after two thousand years, has lost none of the freshness of its beginnings and feels drawn by the Spirit of God to "set out into the deep" (*duc in altum!*) in order once more to proclaim, and even cry out, before the world that Jesus Christ is Lord and Savior, "the way, and the truth, and the life" (John 14:6), "the goal of human history and the point on which the desires of history and civilization turn."

The Rosary, though clearly Marian in character, is at heart a Christocentric prayer. In the sobriety of its elements, it has all the *depth of the Gospel message in its entirety*, of which it can be said to be a compendium. It is an echo of the prayer of Mary, her perennial *Magnificat* for the work of the redemptive Incarnation which began in her virginal womb. With the Rosary, the Christian people *sits at the school of Mary* and is led to contemplate the beauty on the face of

Christ and to experience the depths of his love. Through the Rosary the faithful receive abundant grace, as though from the very hands of the Mother of the Redeemer. . . .

The contemplation of Christ has an *incomparable model* in Mary. In a unique way the face of the Son belongs to Mary. It was in her womb that Christ was formed, receiving from her a human resemblance which points to an even greater spiritual closeness. No one has ever devoted himself to the contemplation of the face of Christ as faithfully as Mary. The eyes of her heart already turned to him at the Annunciation, when she conceived him by the power of the Holy Spirit. In the months that followed she began to sense his presence and to picture his features. When at last she gave birth to him in Bethlehem, her eyes were able to gaze tenderly on the face of her Son, as she "wrapped him in swaddling clothes, and laid him in a manger" (Luke 2:7).

Thereafter Mary's gaze, ever filled with adoration and wonder, would never leave him. At times it would be *a questioning look*, as in the episode of the finding in the Temple: "Son, why have you treated us so?" (Luke 2:48); it would always be *a penetrating gaze*, one capable of deeply understanding Jesus, even to the point of perceiving his hidden feelings and anticipating his decisions, as at Cana (John 2:5). At other times it would be *a look of sorrow*, especially beneath the Cross, where her vision would still be that of a mother giving birth, for Mary not only shared the passion and death of her Son, she also received the new son given to her in the beloved disciple (John 19:26–27). On the morning of Easter hers would be *a gaze radiant with the joy of the Resurrection*, and finally, on the day of Pentecost, *a gaze afire* with the outpouring of the Spirit (Acts 1:14).

Mary lived with her eyes fixed on Christ, treasuring his every word: "She kept all these things, pondering them in her heart"

(Luke 2:19; cf. 2:51). The memories of Jesus, impressed upon her heart, were always with her, leading her to reflect on the various moments of her life at her Son's side. In a way those memories were to be the "rosary" which she recited uninterruptedly throughout her earthly life.

Even now, amid the joyful songs of the heavenly Jerusalem, the reasons for her thanksgiving and praise remain unchanged. They inspire her maternal concern for the pilgrim Church, in which she continues to relate her personal account of the Gospel. *Mary constantly sets before the faithful the "mysteries" of her Son*, with the desire that the contemplation of those mysteries will release all their saving power. In the recitation of the Rosary, the Christian community enters into contact with the memories and the contemplative gaze of Mary.

The Rosary, precisely because it starts with Mary's own experience, is an *exquisitely contemplative prayer*. Without this contemplative dimension, it would lose its meaning, as Pope Paul VI clearly pointed out: "Without contemplation, the Rosary is a body without a soul, and its recitation runs the risk of becoming a mechanical repetition of formulas, in violation of the admonition of Christ: 'In praying do not heap up empty phrases as the Gentiles do; for they think they will be heard for their many words' (Matt. 6:7). By its nature the recitation of the Rosary calls for a quiet rhythm and a lingering pace, helping the individual to meditate on the mysteries of the Lord's life as seen through the eyes of her who was closest to the Lord. In this way the unfathomable riches of these mysteries are disclosed." . . .

Meditation on the mysteries of Christ is proposed in the Rosary by means of a method designed to assist in their assimilation. It is a method *based on repetition*. This applies above all to the *Hail Mary*, repeated ten times in each mystery. If this repetition is considered superficially, there could be a temptation to see the Rosary as a dry and boring exercise. It is quite another thing, however, when the Rosary is thought of as an outpouring of that love which tirelessly returns to the person loved with expressions similar in their content but ever fresh in terms of the feeling pervading them.

In Christ, God has truly assumed a "heart of flesh." Not only does God have a divine heart, rich in mercy and in forgiveness, but also a human heart, capable of all the stirrings of affection. If we needed evidence for this from the Gospel, we could easily find it in the touching dialogue between Christ and Peter after the Resurrection: "Simon, son of John, do you love me?" Three times this question is put to Peter, and three times he gives the reply: "Lord, you know that I love you" (John 21:15–17). Over and above the specific meaning of this passage, so important for Peter's mission, none can fail to recognize the beauty of this triple repetition, in which the insistent request and the corresponding reply are expressed in terms familiar from the universal experience of human love. To understand the Rosary, one has to enter into the psychological dynamic proper to love.

One thing is clear: although the repeated *Hail Mary* is addressed directly to Mary, it is to Jesus that the act of love is ultimately directed, with her and through her. The repetition is nourished by the desire to be conformed ever more completely to Christ, the true program of the Christian life. Saint Paul expressed this project with words of fire: "For me to live is Christ and to die is gain" (Phil. 1:21). And again: "It is no longer I that live, but Christ lives in me" (Gal. 2:20). The Rosary helps us to be conformed ever more closely to Christ until we attain true holiness.

Pope John Paul II, *Rosarium Virginis Mariae*, 1, 10–12, 26, apostolic letter, Vatican website, October 16, 2002, http://www.vatican.va/content/john-paul-ii/en/apost_letters/2002/documents/hf_jp-ii_apl_20021016_rosarium-virginis-mariae.html.

How to Pray the Rosary

.... † ....

Bishop Robert Barron

The Rosary prayer actually consists of a series of smaller prayers, all of which take about twenty minutes to pray. In this brief introduction, we will walk through them together; however, all the necessary prayers also appear in each of the four major sections in this book.

First, you hold the rosary and begin with the sign of the cross:

> *In the name of the Father, and of the Son, and of the Holy Spirit. Amen.*

Next, holding the crucifix of the rosary, you pray the ancient Apostles' Creed, which is a summary of our baptismal promises:

> *I believe in God,*
> *the Father almighty,*
> *Creator of heaven and earth,*
> *and in Jesus Christ, his only Son, our Lord,*
> *who was conceived by the Holy Spirit,*
> *born of the Virgin Mary,*
> *suffered under Pontius Pilate,*

was crucified, died, and was buried;
he descended into hell;
on the third day he rose again from the dead;
he ascended into heaven,
and is seated at the right hand of God the Father almighty;
from there he will come to judge the living and the dead.

I believe in the Holy Spirit,
the holy catholic Church,
the communion of saints,
the forgiveness of sins,
the resurrection of the body,
and life everlasting. Amen.

Holding the first bead above the crucifix, you then pray the Our Father, which is the prayer that Jesus taught us to pray:

Our Father, who art in heaven,
hallowed be thy name;
thy kingdom come,
thy will be done
on earth as it is in heaven.
Give us this day our daily bread,
and forgive us our trespasses,
as we forgive those who trespass against us;
and lead us not into temptation,
but deliver us from evil. Amen.

For each of the three beads that follow, you pray the Hail Mary, which is derived, in part, from the greetings of the angel Gabriel and Mary's relative Elizabeth in Scripture (Luke 1:28, 42). (One thing we might pray for during this introductory triplet is an increase in faith, hope, and love.)

> *Hail Mary, full of grace, the Lord is with thee;*
> *blessed art thou among women,*
> *and blessed is the fruit of thy womb, Jesus.*
> *Holy Mary, Mother of God,*
> *pray for us sinners,*
> *now and at the hour of our death. Amen.*

Next, you pray the Glory Be, which gives praise to the three persons of our one God:

> *Glory be to the Father, and to the Son, and to the Holy Spirit;*
> *as it was in the beginning, is now, and ever shall be,*
> *world without end. Amen.*

Next, we move into the heart of the Rosary—the five "decades." These are groupings of ten beads separated by an individual bead. Each of these decades corresponds to a "mystery" in the lives of Christ and his mother. When you pray the Rosary, you pray it following one of four categories of mysteries: the Joyful Mysteries, the Sorrowful Mysteries, the Glorious Mysteries, and the Luminous Mysteries. Each of the four major sections of this book walk you through the Rosary based on one of these sets of mysteries.

The Joyful Mysteries, which are traditionally prayed on Mondays, Saturdays, and, during the season of Advent, on Sundays, are:

1. THE ANNUNCIATION
2. THE VISITATION
3. THE NATIVITY
4. THE PRESENTATION IN THE TEMPLE
5. THE FINDING IN THE TEMPLE

The Sorrowful Mysteries, which are traditionally prayed on Tuesdays, Fridays, and, during the season of Lent, on Sundays, are:

1. THE AGONY IN THE GARDEN
2. THE SCOURGING AT THE PILLAR
3. THE CROWNING WITH THORNS
4. THE CARRYING OF THE CROSS
5. THE CRUCIFIXION AND DEATH

The Glorious Mysteries, which are traditionally prayed on Wednesdays and, outside the seasons of Advent and Lent, on Sundays, are:

1. THE RESURRECTION
2. THE ASCENSION
3. THE DESCENT OF THE HOLY SPIRIT
4. THE ASSUMPTION
5. THE CORONATION OF MARY

The Joyful Mysteries

.... † ....

OPENING PRAYERS

THE SIGN OF THE CROSS

*In the name of the Father, and of the Son, and of the Holy
Spirit. Amen.*

THE APOSTLES' CREED

*I believe in God,
the Father almighty,
Creator of heaven and earth,
and in Jesus Christ, his only Son, our Lord,
who was conceived by the Holy Spirit,
born of the Virgin Mary,
suffered under Pontius Pilate,
was crucified, died, and was buried;
he descended into hell;
on the third day he rose again from the dead;
he ascended into heaven,
and is seated at the right hand of God the Father almighty;
from there he will come to judge the living and the dead.*

*I believe in the Holy Spirit,
the holy catholic Church,
the communion of saints,
the forgiveness of sins,
the resurrection of the body,*

and life everlasting.
Amen.

THE OUR FATHER

Our Father, who art in heaven,
hallowed be thy name;
thy kingdom come,
thy will be done
on earth as it is in heaven.
Give us this day our daily bread,
and forgive us our trespasses,
as we forgive those who trespass against us;
and lead us not into temptation,
but deliver us from evil.
Amen.

THE HAIL MARY (*three times*)

Hail Mary, full of grace, the Lord is with thee;
blessed art thou among women,
and blessed is the fruit of thy womb, Jesus.
Holy Mary, Mother of God,
pray for us sinners,
now and at the hour of our death. Amen.

THE GLORY BE

Glory be to the Father, and to the Son, and to the Holy Spirit;
as it was in the beginning, is now, and ever shall be,
world without end. Amen.

The First Joyful Mystery

The Annunciation

The Annunciation

REFLECTION
(*Long Option*)

The Annunciation focuses on the most elevated creature: Mary, the Virgin Mother of God. The angel's greeting to Mary is important: "Hail Mary, full of grace." Mary is being addressed as someone who is able to accept gifts, who is ready to receive. Then the angel announces to the maid of Nazareth that she has been chosen to be the Mother of God. Here is what Gabriel says: "Behold, you will conceive in your womb and bear a son, and you shall name him Jesus. He will be great and will be called Son of the Most High, and the Lord God will give him the throne of David his father, and he will rule over the house of Jacob forever, and of his kingdom there will be no end." No first-century Israelite would have missed the meaning here: this child shall be the fulfillment of the promise made to King David. And this means that the child is, in fact, the King of the world, the one who would bring unity and peace to all the nations. The conviction grew upon Israel that this mysterious descendent of David would be King, not just for a time and not just in an earthly sense, but forever and for all nations. This definitive King of the Jews would be King of the world. He would be our King, as well.

As we pray this decade, let us contemplate how we have allowed Jesus to be the King and Lord over our whole life.

REFLECTION
(*Short Option*)

The angel Gabriel announces to Mary that she has been chosen to become the Mother of God. This child, Jesus, would be the fulfillment of the promise made to King David, ruling forever and for all nations.

THE OUR FATHER

> *Our Father, who art in heaven,*
> *hallowed be thy name;*
> *thy kingdom come,*
> *thy will be done*
> *on earth as it is in heaven.*
> *Give us this day our daily bread,*
> *and forgive us our trespasses,*
> *as we forgive those who trespass against us;*
> *and lead us not into temptation,*
> *but deliver us from evil. Amen.*

THE HAIL MARY (*ten times*)

> *Hail Mary, full of grace, the Lord is with thee;*
> *blessed art thou among women,*
> *and blessed is the fruit of thy womb, Jesus.*
> *Holy Mary, Mother of God,*
> *pray for us sinners,*
> *now and at the hour of our death. Amen.*

THE GLORY BE

> *Glory be to the Father, and to the Son, and to the Holy Spirit;*
> *as it was in the beginning, is now, and ever shall be,*
> *world without end. Amen.*

THE FATIMA PRAYER

> *O my Jesus, forgive us our sins, save us from the fires of hell;*
> *lead all souls to heaven, especially those most in need of thy*
> *mercy.*

The Second Joyful Mystery

The Visitation

The Visitation

REFLECTION
(*Long Option*)

Upon hearing the message of Gabriel concerning her own pregnancy and that of her cousin, Mary, we hear, "proceeded in haste into the hill country of Judah" to see Elizabeth.

Why did she go with such speed and purpose? Because she had found her mission, her role in the theo-drama. We are dominated today by the ego-drama in all of its ramifications and implications. The ego-drama is the play that I'm writing, I'm producing, I'm directing, and above all, that I'm starring in. We see this absolutely everywhere in our culture. Freedom of choice reigns supreme: I become the person that I choose to be. But the theo-drama is the great story being told by God, the great play being directed by God. What makes life thrilling is to discover your role in it. This is precisely what has happened to Mary. She has found her role—indeed a climactic role—in the theo-drama, and she wants to commune with Elizabeth, who has also discovered her role in that same drama.

Throughout this decade of the Rosary, let us contemplate what God reveals to us in the mystery of the Visitation. Have we searched for our place in God's story, abandoning the ego-drama for the theo-drama with a response as bold and simple as Mary's?

REFLECTION
(*Short Option*)

U pon hearing the message of Gabriel, Mary "proceeded in haste" to see Elizabeth. Why did she go with such speed and purpose? Because she had found her mission, her role in the great story being told by God.

THE OUR FATHER

> *Our Father, who art in heaven,*
> *hallowed be thy name;*
> *thy kingdom come,*
> *thy will be done*
> *on earth as it is in heaven.*
> *Give us this day our daily bread,*
> *and forgive us our trespasses,*
> *as we forgive those who trespass against us;*
> *and lead us not into temptation,*
> *but deliver us from evil. Amen.*

THE HAIL MARY (*ten times*)

> *Hail Mary, full of grace, the Lord is with thee;*
> *blessed art thou among women,*
> *and blessed is the fruit of thy womb, Jesus.*
> *Holy Mary, Mother of God,*
> *pray for us sinners,*
> *now and at the hour of our death. Amen.*

THE GLORY BE

*Glory be to the Father, and to the Son, and to the Holy Spirit;
as it was in the beginning, is now, and ever shall be,
world without end. Amen.*

THE FATIMA PRAYER

*O my Jesus, forgive us our sins, save us from the fires of hell;
lead all souls to heaven, especially those most in need of thy
mercy.*

The Third Joyful Mystery

The Nativity

The Nativity

REFLECTION
(*Long Option*)

W hen we turn to Luke's familiar account of the birth of Jesus, we see that it commences, as one would expect poems and histories in the ancient world to commence, with the invocation of powerful and important people: Emperor Augustus and Quirinius, the governor of Syria. But then Luke pulls the rug out from under us, for we promptly learn that the story isn't about Augustus and Quirinius at all, but rather about two nobodies making their way from one forgotten outpost of Augustus' empire to another. When Mary and Joseph arrived in David's city, there was no room, even at the crude travelers' hostel, and so their child is born in a cave, or as some scholars have recently suggested, the lower level of a dwelling, the humble part of the house where the animals spent the night.

Luke therefore sets up his story as the tale of two rival emperors: Caesar, the king of the world, and Jesus, the baby King. While Caesar rules from his palace in Rome, Jesus has no place to lay his head; while Caesar exercises rangy power, Jesus is wrapped in swaddling clothes; while Caesar surrounds himself with wealthy and sophisticated courtiers, Jesus is surrounded by animals and shepherds of the field. And yet, the baby King is more powerful than Augustus, which is signaled by the presence of an army (*stratias* in the Greek) of angels in the skies over Bethlehem. All four of the Gospels play out as a struggle, culminating in the deadly business of the cross, between the worldly powers and the power of Christ. For Jesus is not simply a kindly prophet with a gentle message of forgiveness;

REFLECTION
(*Short Option*)

Joseph and Mary bring the infant Jesus into the temple, the dwelling place of the Lord, fulfilling the prophecy that the glory of Yahweh would return to his temple.

THE OUR FATHER

> *Our Father, who art in heaven,*
> *hallowed be thy name;*
> *thy kingdom come,*
> *thy will be done*
> *on earth as it is in heaven.*
> *Give us this day our daily bread,*
> *and forgive us our trespasses,*
> *as we forgive those who trespass against us;*
> *and lead us not into temptation,*
> *but deliver us from evil. Amen.*

THE HAIL MARY (*ten times*)

> *Hail Mary, full of grace, the Lord is with thee;*
> *blessed art thou among women,*
> *and blessed is the fruit of thy womb, Jesus.*
> *Holy Mary, Mother of God,*
> *pray for us sinners,*
> *now and at the hour of our death. Amen.*

THE GLORY BE

> *Glory be to the Father, and to the Son, and to the Holy Spirit;*
> *as it was in the beginning, is now, and ever shall be,*
> *world without end. Amen.*

THE FATIMA PRAYER

> *O my Jesus, forgive us our sins, save us from the fires of hell;*
> *lead all souls to heaven, especially those most in need of thy*
> *mercy.*

The Fifth Joyful Mystery

✝

The Finding in the Temple

The Finding in the Temple

REFLECTION
(*Long Option*)

After their visit to Jerusalem, Mary and Joseph, along with a bevy of their family and friends, were heading home to Nazareth. They presumed that the child Jesus was somewhere among his relatives in the caravan. Instead, he was in the temple of the Lord, conversing with the elders and masters of the Law. Distraught, Mary and Joseph spent three days looking for him. Any parent who has ever searched for a lost child knows the anguish they must have felt. Can you imagine what it was like as they tried to sleep at night, spinning out the worst scenarios in their minds?

When they finally find him, they, with understandable exasperation, upbraid him: "Child, why have you treated us like this? Look, your father and I have been searching for you in great anxiety." But Jesus responds with a kind of devastating laconicism: "Why were you searching for me? Did you not know that I must be in my Father's house?"

The story conveys a truth that runs sharply counter to our sensibilities: even the most powerful familial emotions must, in the end, give way to mission. Though she felt an enormous pull in the opposite direction, Mary let her son go, allowing him to find his.

As we pray the final decade of the Rosary, let us contemplate the paradox at the heart of this joyful mystery: that precisely in the measure that everyone in the family focuses on God's call for one another, the family becomes more loving and peaceful.

REFLECTION
(*Short Option*)

After three days looking for him, Mary and Joseph find the young Jesus in the temple. Jesus says, "Did you not know that I must be in my Father's house?"—conveying that familial emotions must give way to mission.

THE OUR FATHER

Our Father, who art in heaven,
hallowed be thy name;
thy kingdom come,
thy will be done
on earth as it is in heaven.
Give us this day our daily bread,
and forgive us our trespasses,
as we forgive those who trespass against us;
and lead us not into temptation,
but deliver us from evil. Amen.

THE HAIL MARY (*ten times*)

Hail Mary, full of grace, the Lord is with thee;
blessed art thou among women,
and blessed is the fruit of thy womb, Jesus.
Holy Mary, Mother of God,
pray for us sinners,
now and at the hour of our death. Amen.

THE GLORY BE

> *Glory be to the Father, and to the Son, and to the Holy Spirit;*
> *as it was in the beginning, is now, and ever shall be,*
> *world without end. Amen.*

THE FATIMA PRAYER

> *O my Jesus, forgive us our sins, save us from the fires of hell;*
> *lead all souls to heaven, especially those most in need of thy*
> *mercy.*

The Joyful Mysteries

.... † ....

CLOSING PRAYERS

HAIL, HOLY QUEEN

Hail, holy Queen, mother of mercy,
our life, our sweetness, and our hope.
To thee do we cry, poor banished children of Eve;
to thee do we send up our sighs,
mourning and weeping in this valley of tears.
Turn, then, most gracious advocate,
thine eyes of mercy toward us;
and after this, our exile,
show unto us the blessed fruit of thy womb, Jesus.
O clement, O loving, O sweet Virgin Mary.
Pray for us, O holy Mother of God,
that we may be made worthy of the promises of Christ.
Amen.

CONCLUDING PRAYER

Let us pray.
O God, whose only begotten Son,
by his life, death, and Resurrection,
has purchased for us the rewards of eternal life,
grant, we beseech thee,
that while meditating on these mysteries
of the most holy Rosary of the Blessed Virgin Mary,
we may imitate what they contain

and obtain what they promise,
through the same Christ our Lord. Amen.

THE SIGN OF THE CROSS

In the name of the Father, and of the Son, and of the Holy Spirit.
Amen.

THE
Sorrowful Mysteries
OF THE ROSARY

The Sorrowful Mysteries

.... † ....

OPENING PRAYERS

THE SIGN OF THE CROSS

> *In the name of the Father, and of the Son, and of the Holy
> Spirit. Amen.*

THE APOSTLES' CREED

> *I believe in God,*
> *the Father almighty,*
> *Creator of heaven and earth,*
> *and in Jesus Christ, his only Son, our Lord,*
> *who was conceived by the Holy Spirit,*
> *born of the Virgin Mary,*
> *suffered under Pontius Pilate,*
> *was crucified, died, and was buried;*
> *he descended into hell;*
> *on the third day he rose again from the dead;*
> *he ascended into heaven,*
> *and is seated at the right hand of God the Father almighty;*
> *from there he will come to judge the living and the dead.*
>
> *I believe in the Holy Spirit,*
> *the holy catholic Church,*
> *the communion of saints,*
> *the forgiveness of sins,*
> *the resurrection of the body,*

and life everlasting.
Amen.

THE OUR FATHER

Our Father, who art in heaven,
hallowed be thy name;
thy kingdom come,
thy will be done
on earth as it is in heaven.
Give us this day our daily bread,
and forgive us our trespasses,
as we forgive those who trespass against us;
and lead us not into temptation,
but deliver us from evil.
Amen.

THE HAIL MARY (*three times*)

Hail Mary, full of grace, the Lord is with thee;
blessed art thou among women,
and blessed is the fruit of thy womb, Jesus.
Holy Mary, Mother of God,
pray for us sinners,
now and at the hour of our death. Amen.

THE GLORY BE

Glory be to the Father, and to the Son, and to the Holy Spirit;
as it was in the beginning, is now, and ever shall be,
world without end. Amen.

The First Sorrowful Mystery

✝

The Agony in the Garden

The Agony in the Garden

In the Garden of Gethsemane, the Son of God enters into the psychological and spiritual space of the sinner. Paul the Apostle says that Christ *became* sin. That's his mission: to bring the light and forgiveness of God into the depths of godforsakenness. He's accompanied only by Peter, James, and John, but even those three closest disciples he ultimately leaves behind. He's "pressed down to the ground"—the great spiritual writers of our tradition interpret this as the sins of the world pressing down upon him—and he sweats blood. Jesus, the very Son of God, enters into the state of alienation from God. He feels the suffering of the lost.

In that state, he offers an anguished prayer: "Father, if you are willing, remove this cup from me." The whole of Jesus' life is a battle against the devil culminating in the cross—and in the garden, the temptation to avoid following God's will is evident.

Yet struggling against every instinct in his body, he demonstrates fortitude, utterly aligning his will to that of the Father: "Yet, not my will but yours be done." Here at the very center of the drama, and from the center of the co-inherence of the divine and human wills, comes this prayer that signals trust in the divine providence.

As we pray this decade, let us see the aching loneliness of Christ in the garden as his entry into the psychological and spiritual space of the sinner, and to see his great prayer in the garden as a guide for our own prayers and the key to lasting joy and peace: "Not my will but yours be done."

REFLECTION

(*Short Option*)

After Pilate sentences Jesus to crucifixion, he has him scourged at the pillar. Jesus, completely acquiescent to the will of his Father, lovingly accepts his suffering to conquer sin and redeem humanity.

THE OUR FATHER

Our Father, who art in heaven,
hallowed be thy name;
thy kingdom come,
thy will be done
on earth as it is in heaven.
Give us this day our daily bread,
and forgive us our trespasses,
as we forgive those who trespass against us;
and lead us not into temptation,
but deliver us from evil. Amen.

THE HAIL MARY (*ten times*)

Hail Mary, full of grace, the Lord is with thee;
blessed art thou among women,
and blessed is the fruit of thy womb, Jesus.
Holy Mary, Mother of God,
pray for us sinners,
now and at the hour of our death. Amen.

THE GLORY BE

Glory be to the Father, and to the Son, and to the Holy Spirit;
as it was in the beginning, is now, and ever shall be,
world without end. Amen.

THE FATIMA PRAYER

O my Jesus, forgive us our sins, save us from the fires of hell;
lead all souls to heaven, especially those most in need of thy
mercy.

The Third Sorrowful Mystery

············ † ············

The Crowning with Thorns

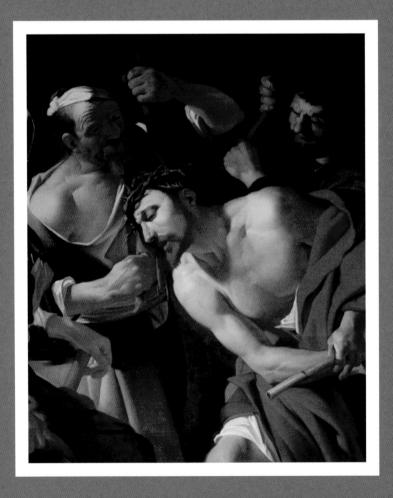

The Crowning with Thorns

REFLECTION
(Long Option)

Upon being presented to Pilate, Jesus is asked: "Are you the King of the Jews?" A blandly affirmative answer comes: "You say so." This leads the Roman soldiers to place a purple military cloak on his shoulders, a reed in his right hand, and a crown of thorns on his head. They say, "Hail, King of the Jews," and they further mock him by kneeling before him, spitting on him, and striking him on the head with the reed.

But Mark's Gospel does not want us to miss the irony that, precisely as the King of the Jews and the Son of David, Jesus is implicitly King to those soldiers, for the mission of the Davidic king is the unification not only of the tribes of Israel but also of the tribes of all the world. In a meditation he wrote on this mystery, Fulton Sheen calls this mockery of the true King by the soldiers—who presume Jesus' kingship to be false—an atonement for the "sins of the mind," such as egotism, doubt, and pride. The key to honor in the kingdom of God is the willingness to suffer out of love, to give one's life away as a gift. Look at the lives of the saints. It is never about aggrandizing the ego but rather emptying it out.

For this decade, let us savor the way that Christ absorbs the mockery and hatred of the crowd, and thereby reveals the quality of the divine forgiveness and love.

REFLECTION
(*Short Option*)

After being scourged and crowned with thorns, Jesus is made to carry his cross. Jesus places this terrible image at the very center of the spiritual life, and we take up our own cross by being willing to suffer as Jesus did.

THE OUR FATHER

> *Our Father, who art in heaven,*
> *hallowed be thy name;*
> *thy kingdom come,*
> *thy will be done*
> *on earth as it is in heaven.*
> *Give us this day our daily bread,*
> *and forgive us our trespasses,*
> *as we forgive those who trespass against us;*
> *and lead us not into temptation,*
> *but deliver us from evil. Amen.*

THE HAIL MARY (*ten times*)

> *Hail Mary, full of grace, the Lord is with thee;*
> *blessed art thou among women,*
> *and blessed is the fruit of thy womb, Jesus.*
> *Holy Mary, Mother of God,*
> *pray for us sinners,*
> *now and at the hour of our death. Amen.*

THE GLORY BE

> *Glory be to the Father, and to the Son, and to the Holy Spirit;*
> *as it was in the beginning, is now, and ever shall be,*
> *world without end. Amen.*

THE FATIMA PRAYER

> *O my Jesus, forgive us our sins, save us from the fires of hell;*
> *lead all souls to heaven, especially those most in need of thy*
> *mercy.*

The Fifth Sorrowful Mystery

The Crucifixion and Death

The Crucifixion and Death

REFLECTION
(Long Option)

Christians have become so accustomed to seeing the crucifix—in churches, in schools, on seasonal greeting cards, or worn as jewelry around people's necks—that they have lost any sense of how awful and strange it is. But to the first Christians, the cross of Christ was that and more. Paul called it "a stumbling block to the Jews and foolishness to Gentiles," insinuating that it was sure to bother just about everybody. For the first several centuries of Christianity, artists were reluctant to depict the death of the Lord because it was just too terrible. And yet, Paul can say, "We proclaim Christ crucified," and the entire Christian tradition—from Augustine to Francis of Assisi to Dante to Ignatius of Loyola to Trappist monks in the hills of Kentucky—has echoed him. Somehow they knew that writhing figure pinned to his cross *is* the whole story.

What is that story? The Crucifixion of Jesus is God's judgment on the world and the fullest expression of the divine anger at sin. We are meant to see on that cross not simply a violent display but rather our own ugliness. What brought Jesus to the cross? Stupidity, anger, mistrust, institutional injustice, betrayal of friends, denial, unspeakable cruelty, scapegoating, and fear. In other words, all of our dysfunction is revealed on that cross. In the light of the cross, no one can honestly say, "I'm okay, and you're okay." In the tormented face of Christ crucified, we know that something has gone terribly wrong with God's creation, that we are like prisoners chained inside of an escape-proof prison, that we are at war with ourselves.

Does this mean God the Father is a cruel taskmaster demanding a bloody sacrifice to appease his anger? No, because we also see something else in the brutality of the cross. We see that God himself has come to stand with us—shoulder to shoulder—in our dysfunction. Jesus' Crucifixion was the opening up of the divine heart so that we could see that no sin of ours could finally separate us from the love of God.

As we pray this final decade, let us savor the strange beauty and the mystery of the crucified Son of God.

REFLECTION
(*Short Option*)

Jesus is brutally crucified. This Crucifixion is the fullest expression of the divine anger at sin. But it is also the opening up of the divine heart so that we could see that no sin of ours could finally separate us from God's love.

THE OUR FATHER

> *Our Father, who art in heaven,*
> *hallowed be thy name;*
> *thy kingdom come,*
> *thy will be done*
> *on earth as it is in heaven.*
> *Give us this day our daily bread,*
> *and forgive us our trespasses,*
> *as we forgive those who trespass against us;*
> *and lead us not into temptation,*
> *but deliver us from evil. Amen.*

THE HAIL MARY (*ten times*)

> *Hail Mary, full of grace, the Lord is with thee;*
> *blessed art thou among women,*
> *and blessed is the fruit of thy womb, Jesus.*
> *Holy Mary, Mother of God,*
> *pray for us sinners,*
> *now and at the hour of our death. Amen.*

THE GLORY BE

> *Glory be to the Father, and to the Son, and to the Holy Spirit;*
> *as it was in the beginning, is now, and ever shall be,*
> *world without end. Amen.*

THE FATIMA PRAYER

> *O my Jesus, forgive us our sins, save us from the fires of hell;*
> *lead all souls to heaven, especially those most in need of thy*
> *mercy.*

The Sorrowful Mysteries

.... † ....

CLOSING PRAYERS

HAIL, HOLY QUEEN

Hail, holy Queen, mother of mercy,
our life, our sweetness, and our hope.
To thee do we cry, poor banished children of Eve;
to thee do we send up our sighs,
mourning and weeping in this valley of tears.
Turn, then, most gracious advocate,
thine eyes of mercy toward us;
and after this, our exile,
show unto us the blessed fruit of thy womb, Jesus.
O clement, O loving, O sweet Virgin Mary.
Pray for us, O holy Mother of God,
that we may be made worthy of the promises of Christ.
Amen.

CONCLUDING PRAYER

Let us pray.
O God, whose only begotten Son,
by his life, death, and Resurrection,
has purchased for us the rewards of eternal life,
grant, we beseech thee,
that while meditating on these mysteries
of the most holy Rosary of the Blessed Virgin Mary,
we may imitate what they contain

and obtain what they promise,
through the same Christ our Lord. Amen.

THE SIGN OF THE CROSS

In the name of the Father, and of the Son, and of the Holy Spirit.
Amen.

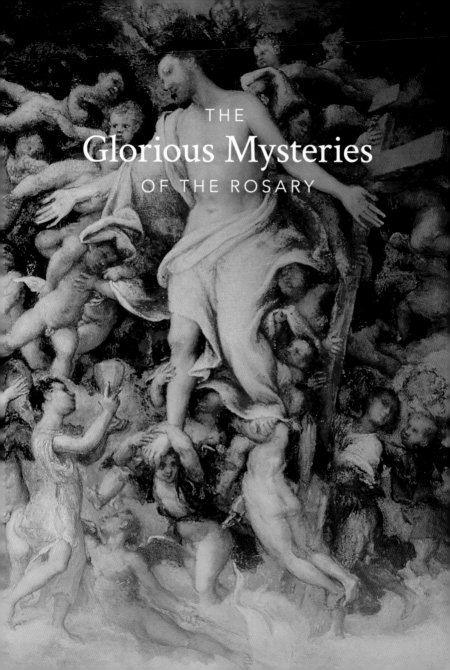

THE
Glorious Mysteries
OF THE ROSARY

The Glorious Mysteries

.... † ....

OPENING PRAYERS

The Sign of the Cross

In the name of the Father, and of the Son, and of the Holy Spirit. Amen.

The Apostles' Creed

I believe in God,
the Father almighty,
Creator of heaven and earth,
and in Jesus Christ, his only Son, our Lord,
who was conceived by the Holy Spirit,
born of the Virgin Mary,
suffered under Pontius Pilate,
was crucified, died, and was buried;
he descended into hell;
on the third day he rose again from the dead;
he ascended into heaven,
and is seated at the right hand of God the Father almighty;
from there he will come to judge the living and the dead.

I believe in the Holy Spirit,
the holy catholic Church,
the communion of saints,
the forgiveness of sins,
the resurrection of the body,

and life everlasting.
Amen.

THE OUR FATHER

Our Father, who art in heaven,
hallowed be thy name;
thy kingdom come,
thy will be done
on earth as it is in heaven.
Give us this day our daily bread,
and forgive us our trespasses,
as we forgive those who trespass against us;
and lead us not into temptation,
but deliver us from evil.
Amen.

THE HAIL MARY (*three times*)

Hail Mary, full of grace, the Lord is with thee;
blessed art thou among women,
and blessed is the fruit of thy womb, Jesus.
Holy Mary, Mother of God,
pray for us sinners,
now and at the hour of our death. Amen.

THE GLORY BE

Glory be to the Father, and to the Son, and to the Holy Spirit;
as it was in the beginning, is now, and ever shall be,
world without end. Amen.

The First Glorious Mystery

***

The Resurrection

The Resurrection

REFLECTION
(*Long Option*)

In John's magnificent account of the Resurrection, he says that it was early in the morning on the first day of the week. It was still dark—just the way it was at the beginning of time before God said, "Let there be light." But a light was about to shine, and a new creation was about to appear.

The stone had been rolled away. That stone, blocking the entrance to the tomb of Jesus after his Passion and Crucifixion, stands for the finality of death. When someone that we love dies, it is as though a great stone is rolled across them, permanently blocking our access to them. And this is why we weep at death—not just in grief but in a kind of existential frustration.

But for Jesus, the stone had been rolled away. What was dreamed about, what endured as a hope against hope, has become a reality. God has opened the grave of his Son, and the bonds of death have been shattered forever. The Resurrection is the clearest indication of the Lordship of Jesus.

The Resurrection reveals certain definite truths. First, that Jesus, having gone all the way down, having journeyed into pain, despair, alienation, death itself, to the limits of godforsakenness, now includes in the divine mercy all those who had wandered far from God. No matter how far we run from the Father, we are always running toward the outstretched arms of the Son.

A second truth is that, in our conflicted world, Christ is not on the side of the scapegoaters but rather on the side of the scapegoated victim. The true God does not sanction a community created through violence; rather, he sanctions what Jesus called the kingdom of God, a society grounded in forgiveness, love, and redemption.

So awed were the disciples by Jesus' victory over death and sin and scapegoating in the Resurrection—and you can sense it in every book and letter of the New Testament—that they awaited the imminent arrival of the new state of affairs, the return of Jesus and the establishment of God's kingdom. The old world was over, broken, compromised, its destruction now just a matter of time.

As we pray this first decade, let us contemplate how much Christ loves us and how his love changes the world.

REFLECTION
(*Short Option*)

Jesus the Lord is raised from the dead, revealing that he has gone to the limits of godforsakenness to reach sinners; that he is on the side of the scapegoated victim; and that the destruction of the old world is just a matter of time.

THE OUR FATHER

> *Our Father, who art in heaven,*
> *hallowed be thy name;*
> *thy kingdom come,*
> *thy will be done*
> *on earth as it is in heaven.*
> *Give us this day our daily bread,*
> *and forgive us our trespasses,*
> *as we forgive those who trespass against us;*
> *and lead us not into temptation,*
> *but deliver us from evil. Amen.*

THE HAIL MARY (*ten times*)

> *Hail Mary, full of grace, the Lord is with thee;*
> *blessed art thou among women,*
> *and blessed is the fruit of thy womb, Jesus.*
> *Holy Mary, Mother of God,*
> *pray for us sinners,*
> *now and at the hour of our death. Amen.*

THE GLORY BE

> *Glory be to the Father, and to the Son, and to the Holy Spirit;*
> *as it was in the beginning, is now, and ever shall be,*
> *world without end. Amen.*

THE FATIMA PRAYER

> *O my Jesus, forgive us our sins, save us from the fires of hell;*
> *lead all souls to heaven, especially those most in need of thy*
> *mercy.*

The Second Glorious Mystery

·········· † ··········

The Ascension

The Ascension

REFLECTION
(Long Option)

After commissioning his disciples—and us—to proclaim the Gospel to the whole world, Jesus ascends to heaven, where he takes his place at God's right hand.

How can we even begin to make sense of this mystery, and what does it have to do with us? When we consider the Ascension, it's important to understand that Jesus has not gone up, up, and away, but rather, if I can put it this way, more deeply into our world. He has gone to a dimension that transcends and yet impinges upon our universe. And the prayer of Jesus is that the earth will be filled with the glory of God, that it will be transformed and elevated according to God's purposes. As Jesus leaves the scene—at least in the most obvious sense—he opens the stage for us, so that we might act in his name and in accord with his Spirit. It is precisely those who are most focused on the things of heaven that do most good here below. Those who pray most intently are most effective in the practical realm. This is opened up by the Ascension.

For this decade, meditate on the great mystery of Jesus' bodily Ascension, which is an invitation for us to go on mission.

REFLECTION
(*Short Option*)

After commissioning his disciples to proclaim the Gospel to the world, Jesus ascends to heaven, simultaneously going more deeply into our world and opening the stage for us to act in his name and in accord with his Spirit.

THE OUR FATHER

> *Our Father, who art in heaven,*
> *hallowed be thy name;*
> *thy kingdom come,*
> *thy will be done*
> *on earth as it is in heaven.*
> *Give us this day our daily bread,*
> *and forgive us our trespasses,*
> *as we forgive those who trespass against us;*
> *and lead us not into temptation,*
> *but deliver us from evil. Amen.*

THE HAIL MARY (*ten times*)

> *Hail Mary, full of grace, the Lord is with thee;*
> *blessed art thou among women,*
> *and blessed is the fruit of thy womb, Jesus.*
> *Holy Mary, Mother of God,*
> *pray for us sinners,*
> *now and at the hour of our death. Amen.*

THE GLORY BE

Glory be to the Father, and to the Son, and to the Holy Spirit;
as it was in the beginning, is now, and ever shall be,
world without end. Amen.

THE FATIMA PRAYER

O my Jesus, forgive us our sins, save us from the fires of hell;
lead all souls to heaven, especially those most in need of thy
mercy.

The Third Glorious Mystery

†

The Descent of the Holy Spirit

The Descent of the Holy Spirit

REFLECTION
(*Long Option*)

After Jesus' Ascension, the disciples—the core of the Church—are gathered in the upper room, where the Holy Spirit descends upon them. The Spirit is not a force or a principle but rather a person, that divine person who is the love shared by the Father and the Son, the love that God is. From that event, timorous and largely uneducated men became fearless evangelists, ready and able to spread the Gospel far and wide.

We get some clues as to the nature of the Holy Spirit from the descriptions offered in the New Testament: wind and flame. The term "Holy Spirit," of course, just means Holy Breath—*Spiritus Sanctus*. Wind is mysterious, blowing where it will, coming and going in unpredictable ways. When you have the Holy Spirit in your life, you are not in control. You cannot command the Spirit to come; you have to wait for him and pray for him, as the disciples are portrayed as doing. And once he arrives, you have to be ready to move according to his prompting.

And the Spirit is like fire. And mind you, not just fire, but tongues of fire. The Holy Spirit, who *is* nothing but communication between the Father and the Son, inspires fiery speech: clear, distinct, and uncompromising speech on behalf of Jesus. And this proclamation is public, not private. The first thing the disciples do once they realize that the fire has fallen upon them is to go out and preach the Gospel.

As we pray this decade of the Rosary, let us contemplate the importance of this mystery for the life of the Church today and ponder our mission to continue boldly and publicly to witness to Jesus Christ.

REFLECTION
(*Short Option*)

After Jesus' Ascension, the disciples are gathered in the upper room, where the Holy Spirit descends upon them, its wind and flames sending them—and us—on a mission of bold and public evangelization.

THE OUR FATHER

> *Our Father, who art in heaven,*
> *hallowed be thy name;*
> *thy kingdom come,*
> *thy will be done*
> *on earth as it is in heaven.*
> *Give us this day our daily bread,*
> *and forgive us our trespasses,*
> *as we forgive those who trespass against us;*
> *and lead us not into temptation,*
> *but deliver us from evil. Amen.*

THE HAIL MARY (*ten times*)

> *Hail Mary, full of grace, the Lord is with thee;*
> *blessed art thou among women,*
> *and blessed is the fruit of thy womb, Jesus.*
> *Holy Mary, Mother of God,*
> *pray for us sinners,*
> *now and at the hour of our death. Amen.*

THE GLORY BE

> *Glory be to the Father, and to the Son, and to the Holy Spirit;*
> *as it was in the beginning, is now, and ever shall be,*
> *world without end. Amen.*

THE FATIMA PRAYER

> *O my Jesus, forgive us our sins, save us from the fires of hell;*
> *lead all souls to heaven, especially those most in need of thy*
> *mercy.*

The Fourth Glorious Mystery

.... ✝ ....

The Assumption

The Assumption

REFLECTION
(Long Option)

The *Catechism of the Catholic Church*, quoting *Lumen Gentium*, teaches that "the Immaculate Virgin, preserved free from all stain of original sin, when the course of her earthly life was finished, was taken up body and soul into heavenly glory." In other words, Mary is the first participant in the fullness of Christ's Resurrection.

In her great *Magnificat*, Mary is the new Isaiah, the new Jeremiah, the new Ezekiel, for she announces with greatest clarity and joy the coming of the Messiah. What was only vaguely foreseen in those great prophetic figures is now in clear focus: "He has shown the strength of his arm; he has scattered the proud in their conceit; he has filled the hungry with good things and the rich he has sent away empty. He has come to the help of his servant Israel, for he has remembered his promise of mercy, the promise he made to our fathers, to Abraham and his children forever." There is nothing stronger or more beautiful in any of the prophets.

But Mary is more than strong and beautiful; she is the sinless one, the perfect disciple. Mary, who exists now in this other world, is not so much *somewhere* else as *somehow* else, and this helps to explain why we can speak of her, especially in her heavenly state, as interceding and praying for us.

For this decade, let us contemplate Mary's critical role in salvation history, culminating in her bodily Assumption, which, like the Ascension of Jesus, draws us toward a higher world.

REFLECTION
(*Short Option*)

As the sinless one and the perfect disciple, Mary is assumed—body and soul—into the dimension of God. She is not so much *somewhere* else as *somehow* else, and intercedes and prays for us in her heavenly state.

THE OUR FATHER

> *Our Father, who art in heaven,*
> *hallowed be thy name;*
> *thy kingdom come,*
> *thy will be done*
> *on earth as it is in heaven.*
> *Give us this day our daily bread,*
> *and forgive us our trespasses,*
> *as we forgive those who trespass against us;*
> *and lead us not into temptation,*
> *but deliver us from evil. Amen.*

THE HAIL MARY (*ten times*)

> *Hail Mary, full of grace, the Lord is with thee;*
> *blessed art thou among women,*
> *and blessed is the fruit of thy womb, Jesus.*
> *Holy Mary, Mother of God,*
> *pray for us sinners,*
> *now and at the hour of our death. Amen.*

THE GLORY BE

> *Glory be to the Father, and to the Son, and to the Holy Spirit;*
> *as it was in the beginning, is now, and ever shall be,*
> *world without end. Amen.*

THE FATIMA PRAYER

> *O my Jesus, forgive us our sins, save us from the fires of hell;*
> *lead all souls to heaven, especially those most in need of thy*
> *mercy.*

The Fifth Glorious Mystery

The Coronation of Mary

The Coronation of Mary

REFLECTION
(*Long Option*)

The *Catechism* also teaches us that Mary, having been assumed body and soul into heaven, is "exalted by the Lord as Queen over all things, so that she might be more fully conformed to her Son, the Lord of lords and conqueror of sin and death."

The Queenship of Mary, however, is far from a sentimental image. One of the great biblical points of reference for the coronation of Mary is the twelfth chapter of the book of Revelation. John the visionary sees "a great portent in heaven: a woman clothed with the sun, with the moon under her feet, and on her head a crown of twelve stars." Clothed with the sun and with the moon under her feet, she is a figure of cosmic significance and power; and crowned, coronated, we know that she is a Queen.

Then we discover that she is a Queen mother, for she was "crying out in birth pangs, in the agony of giving birth." Next, we learn that this cosmic Queen mother is also a warrior: "Another portent appeared in heaven; a great red dragon, with seven heads and ten horns. . . . The dragon stood before the woman, who was about to bear a child so that he might devour her child as soon as it was born." What does the red dragon symbolize? Rooted in references from Psalm 89, from the prophet Isaiah, and from the book Genesis, the red dragon is a sort of summation of all of the forces that stand opposed to God and God's creative intention for the human race. He stands athwart the woman and her son.

After the woman's child is born, the son is snatched away, and then a great war breaks out in heaven: Michael and his angels against the dragon and his angels, and the enemy is thrown down. What is being portrayed here, in beautifully vivid language, is the fact that the Queen of Heaven and her Son are the victors in a great cosmic struggle. They embody the victory of God over the forces of chaos, violence, hatred, cruelty, oppression, and injustice.

As we pray this last decade, contemplate the coronation of Mary in heaven—not as a sentimental ceremony, but as a dramatic and subversive mystery, the total victory of God in Christ.

REFLECTION
(Short Option)

After being assumed body and soul into heaven, Mary is crowned by the Lord as Queen over all things. This is not a sentimental ceremony but a dramatic and subversive mystery, the total victory of God in Christ.

THE OUR FATHER

> *Our Father, who art in heaven,*
> *hallowed be thy name;*
> *thy kingdom come,*
> *thy will be done*
> *on earth as it is in heaven.*
> *Give us this day our daily bread,*
> *and forgive us our trespasses,*
> *as we forgive those who trespass against us;*
> *and lead us not into temptation,*
> *but deliver us from evil. Amen.*

THE HAIL MARY (*ten times*)

> *Hail Mary, full of grace, the Lord is with thee;*
> *blessed art thou among women,*
> *and blessed is the fruit of thy womb, Jesus.*
> *Holy Mary, Mother of God,*
> *pray for us sinners,*
> *now and at the hour of our death. Amen.*

THE GLORY BE

> *Glory be to the Father, and to the Son, and to the Holy Spirit;*
> *as it was in the beginning, is now, and ever shall be,*
> *world without end. Amen.*

THE FATIMA PRAYER

> *O my Jesus, forgive us our sins, save us from the fires of hell;*
> *lead all souls to heaven, especially those most in need of thy*
> *mercy.*

The Glorious Mysteries

.... † ....

CLOSING PRAYERS

HAIL, HOLY QUEEN

> *Hail, holy Queen, mother of mercy,*
> *our life, our sweetness, and our hope.*
> *To thee do we cry, poor banished children of Eve;*
> *to thee do we send up our sighs,*
> *mourning and weeping in this valley of tears.*
> *Turn, then, most gracious advocate,*
> *thine eyes of mercy toward us;*
> *and after this, our exile,*
> *show unto us the blessed fruit of thy womb, Jesus.*
> *O clement, O loving, O sweet Virgin Mary.*
> *Pray for us, O holy Mother of God,*
> *that we may be made worthy of the promises of Christ.*
> *Amen.*

CONCLUDING PRAYER

> *Let us pray.*
> *O God, whose only begotten Son,*
> *by his life, death, and Resurrection,*
> *has purchased for us the rewards of eternal life,*
> *grant, we beseech thee,*
> *that while meditating on these mysteries*
> *of the most holy Rosary of the Blessed Virgin Mary,*
> *we may imitate what they contain*

and obtain what they promise,
through the same Christ our Lord. Amen.

THE SIGN OF THE CROSS

In the name of the Father, and of the Son, and of the Holy Spirit.
Amen.

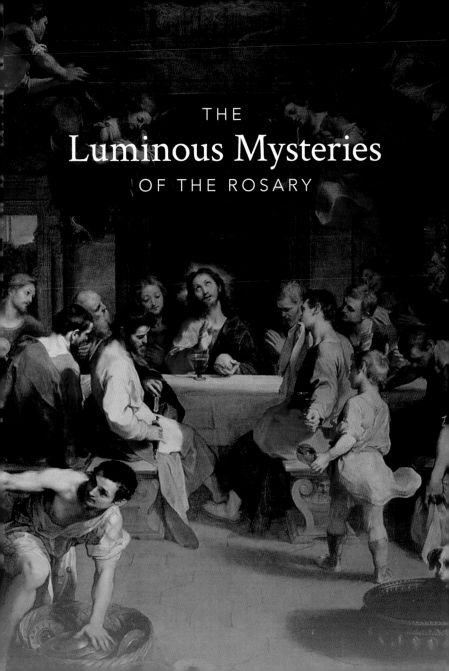

THE
Luminous Mysteries
OF THE ROSARY

The First Luminous Mystery

✝

The Baptism of Christ in the Jordan

The Baptism of Christ in the Jordan

REFLECTION
(*Long Option*)

How strange and scandalous seems the baptism of Jesus. Christ the Lord, the Messiah, the Son of God, the sinless Lamb who takes away the sins of the world, receives for himself the baptism of John, a baptism of repentance. Why is Jesus seeking a baptism of repentance? The difficulty is reflected in the Baptist's confusion: "I should be baptized by you; and yet you come to me." It cannot be true that the Lord Jesus is a sinner, because if this is true, all of Christian revelation is undermined.

As is usually the case with the Bible, what we have here is a startling surprise. Before ever a word passes Jesus' lips, he is presenting his mission. In this gesture, God lays aside his glory and humbly joins us in the muddy waters of our sinfulness. Though sinless, Christ stands with us. Though we are sinners, Christ does not remain aloof. Jesus says, "Give in for now. We must do this to fulfill all righteousness." Fulfilling righteousness, in the old dispensation, would have meant something like "doing what God wants," or "getting right with God." Yet God in Christ takes this a step further. Now we see that "all righteousness" has to do with God's setting things right with us and for us by humbly standing with the sinners he means to save.

As we pray this first decade, let us contemplate our own Baptism, which unites us to the Lamb of God, who takes away the sins of the world.

REFLECTION
(*Short Option*)

At the wedding feast at Cana, Jesus changes 180 gallons of water into the wine of the divine life—an intoxication of grace! When we are infused with the divine life, when we are married to God, life never runs out.

THE OUR FATHER

> *Our Father, who art in heaven,*
> *hallowed be thy name;*
> *thy kingdom come,*
> *thy will be done*
> *on earth as it is in heaven.*
> *Give us this day our daily bread,*
> *and forgive us our trespasses,*
> *as we forgive those who trespass against us;*
> *and lead us not into temptation,*
> *but deliver us from evil. Amen.*

THE HAIL MARY (*ten times*)

> *Hail Mary, full of grace, the Lord is with thee;*
> *blessed art thou among women,*
> *and blessed is the fruit of thy womb, Jesus.*
> *Holy Mary, Mother of God,*
> *pray for us sinners,*
> *now and at the hour of our death. Amen.*

THE GLORY BE

*Glory be to the Father, and to the Son, and to the Holy Spirit;
as it was in the beginning, is now, and ever shall be,
world without end. Amen.*

THE FATIMA PRAYER

*O my Jesus, forgive us our sins, save us from the fires of hell;
lead all souls to heaven, especially those most in need of thy
mercy.*

The Third Luminous Mystery

Jesus' Proclamation of the Coming of the Kingdom of God

Jesus' Proclamation of the Coming of the Kingdom of God

REFLECTION
(*Long Option*)

The first words out of the mouth of Jesus in the Gospel of Mark are a call to conversion: "The kingdom of God has come near. Repent and believe in the Good News." Let's take a closer look at the invitation Christ places on offer.

First, *repent*. Notice that the life, preaching, and mission of Jesus are predicated upon the assumption that all is not well with us. A salvation religion makes no sense if we're all basically fine, if all we need is a little sprucing up around the edges. Christian saints are those who can bear the awful revelation that sin is not simply an abstraction or something that other people wrestle with but a power that lurks and works in them.

Second, *believe in the Good News*. Something here is being brought to completion. What is it? It is the story of Israel itself. Jesus fulfills in his person the entirety of the Old Testament and this is why his presence is so compelling and why following him is of paramount importance. The Good News is he himself, and it's time to make a decision. When Jesus calls, we have to respond—the time is now.

As we pray this decade, let us contemplate Jesus' proclamation of the coming of the kingdom of God as the inbreaking of a new world, one that commands us to change our way of thinking and acting.

REFLECTION
(*Short Option*)

Jesus' first words in the Gospel of Mark are: "The kingdom of God has come near. Repent and believe in the Good News." This proclamation is the inbreaking of a new world, one that changes our way of thinking and acting.

THE OUR FATHER

Our Father, who art in heaven,
hallowed be thy name;
thy kingdom come,
thy will be done
on earth as it is in heaven.
Give us this day our daily bread,
and forgive us our trespasses,
as we forgive those who trespass against us;
and lead us not into temptation,
but deliver us from evil. Amen.

THE HAIL MARY (*ten times*)

Hail Mary, full of grace, the Lord is with thee;
blessed art thou among women,
and blessed is the fruit of thy womb, Jesus.
Holy Mary, Mother of God,
pray for us sinners,
now and at the hour of our death. Amen.

THE GLORY BE

Glory be to the Father, and to the Son, and to the Holy Spirit; as it was in the beginning, is now, and ever shall be, world without end. Amen.

THE FATIMA PRAYER

O my Jesus, forgive us our sins, save us from the fires of hell; lead all souls to heaven, especially those most in need of thy mercy.

The Fourth Luminous Mystery

†

The Transfiguration

The Transfiguration

REFLECTION
(*Long Option*)

Jesus goes up the mountain with Peter, James, and John. This seemingly ordinary man from Nazareth, this brother of theirs, this fellow Israelite, is then transfigured before them, his face shining like the sun and his clothes becoming white as light. The Greek term behind our word "transfiguration" is *metamorphoō* (to go beyond the form that you have). The metamorphosis of a caterpillar comes to mind. This ordinary Jesus—and there is no indication that they have lost sight of who it was—somehow became transformed, elevated, enhanced in his manner of being.

The first thing we notice is that his appearance became more beautiful. One of the classical features of beauty is *claritas* or radiance: his face "shone" and his clothes became "white as light." The proximity of his divinity in no way compromises the integrity of his humanity but rather makes it shine in greater beauty. These somewhat grubby bodies of ours—whose beauty lasts for a fleeting moment—are destined for a transfigured, elevated beauty.

Secondly, in his transfigured state, Jesus transcends space and time, since he is pictured talking with Moses and Elijah, figures representing the Law and the prophets of the Old Testament. In this world, we are caught in one moment of space and time, but in heaven, we will live in the eternal now of God's life—a higher, richer, more beautiful, and spiritually fulfilling life awaits us.

For this decade, think about how the mystery of the Transfiguration doesn't just reveal who Christ is—it reveals who we sinners are called to become: eternal sons and daughters of the living God.

REFLECTION
(*Short Option*)

Jesus goes up the mountain with Peter, James, and John and is beautifully transfigured before them. This reveals not only who Christ is but who we sinners are called to become: eternal sons and daughters of the living God.

THE OUR FATHER

Our Father, who art in heaven,
hallowed be thy name;
thy kingdom come,
thy will be done
on earth as it is in heaven.
Give us this day our daily bread,
and forgive us our trespasses,
as we forgive those who trespass against us;
and lead us not into temptation,
but deliver us from evil. Amen.

THE HAIL MARY (*ten times*)

Hail Mary, full of grace, the Lord is with thee;
blessed art thou among women,
and blessed is the fruit of thy womb, Jesus.
Holy Mary, Mother of God,
pray for us sinners,
now and at the hour of our death. Amen.

THE GLORY BE

> *Glory be to the Father, and to the Son, and to the Holy Spirit;*
> *as it was in the beginning, is now, and ever shall be,*
> *world without end. Amen.*

THE FATIMA PRAYER

> *O my Jesus, forgive us our sins, save us from the fires of hell;*
> *lead all souls to heaven, especially those most in need of thy*
> *mercy.*

The Fifth Luminous Mystery

······ † ······

The Institution of the Eucharist

The Institution of the Eucharist

REFLECTION
(Long Option)

J esus asks his disciples to go into Jerusalem and prepare a Passover supper. The Eucharist is, first, the great meal of fellowship that God wants to establish with his people, the joyful bond in which the divine life is shared spiritually and physically with a hungry world.

However, in a fallen world, this communion is impossible without sacrifice. At the heart of the Passover meal was the eating of a sacrificed lamb in remembrance of the lambs of the original Passover whose blood had been smeared on the doorposts of the Israelites in Egypt. Making his Last Supper a Passover meal, Jesus was signaling the fulfillment of John the Baptist's prophecy that he, Jesus, would be the definitive Lamb of God. This emphasis becomes even clearer when we meditate on the image of the disciples drinking the blood of Jesus from a cup. When someone came to the temple to offer sacrifice, he would cut the throat of the animal, and a priest would catch the victim's blood in a cup before carrying it in for the offering. The implication is clear: Jesus is referring to his own blood being shed for the forgiveness of sins.

After blessing and breaking the unleavened bread of the Passover meal, Jesus pronounced these words: "Take and eat; this is my body." The central claim of the Catholic Church is that Jesus is substantially present under the forms of bread and wine, and that this definitive sacrifice is made sacramentally present at every Mass. His presence is not simply evocative and symbolic but rather real, true, substantial. If Jesus were simply an ordinary human being, his words would have, at best, a symbolic resonance. But Jesus is God, and what God says, is.

As we pray this final decade, meditate on Christ's institution of the Eucharist as a great meal of fellowship, the definitive sacrifice, and the Real Presence under the forms of bread and wine. The Eucharist is the Lord Jesus himself.

REFLECTION
(*Short Option*)

Jesus institutes the definitive sacrifice of the Eucharist at the heart of a Passover meal, making himself really and truly present under the forms of bread and wine.

THE OUR FATHER

Our Father, who art in heaven,
hallowed be thy name;
thy kingdom come,
thy will be done
on earth as it is in heaven.
Give us this day our daily bread,
and forgive us our trespasses,
as we forgive those who trespass against us;
and lead us not into temptation,
but deliver us from evil. Amen.

THE HAIL MARY (*ten times*)

Hail Mary, full of grace, the Lord is with thee;
blessed art thou among women,
and blessed is the fruit of thy womb, Jesus.

Holy Mary, Mother of God,
pray for us sinners,
now and at the hour of our death. Amen.

THE GLORY BE

Glory be to the Father, and to the Son, and to the Holy Spirit;
as it was in the beginning, is now, and ever shall be,
world without end. Amen.

THE FATIMA PRAYER

O my Jesus, forgive us our sins, save us from the fires of hell;
lead all souls to heaven, especially those most in need of thy
mercy.

The Luminous Mysteries

.... † ....

CLOSING PRAYERS

HAIL, HOLY QUEEN

Hail, holy Queen, mother of mercy,
our life, our sweetness, and our hope.
To thee do we cry, poor banished children of Eve;
to thee do we send up our sighs,
mourning and weeping in this valley of tears.
Turn, then, most gracious advocate,
thine eyes of mercy toward us;
and after this, our exile,
show unto us the blessed fruit of thy womb, Jesus.
O clement, O loving, O sweet Virgin Mary.
Pray for us, O holy Mother of God,
that we may be made worthy of the promises of Christ.
Amen.

CONCLUDING PRAYER

Let us pray.
O God, whose only begotten Son,
by his life, death, and Resurrection,
has purchased for us the rewards of eternal life,
grant, we beseech thee,
that while meditating on these mysteries
of the most holy Rosary of the Blessed Virgin Mary,
we may imitate what they contain

and obtain what they promise,
through the same Christ our Lord. Amen.

THE SIGN OF THE CROSS

In the name of the Father, and of the Son, and of the Holy Spirit.
Amen.

Seeing Mary as She Is

.... † ....

Matt Nelson

People treat a thing according to what they think it is. The first test of sanity is whether or not someone *sees* what is really there. The second test of sanity is whether or not someone *acts* according to what is really there. What we see and how we act ultimately determines whether we're living "in the real world" or not.

Mary is a real person—and she's your mother and mine. Take a moment to think about this. You know it; but do you live as though you know it? Do you see Mary—and treat her—*as she really is?*

I'm afraid I often don't. Admittedly, I often get so caught up in studying and contemplating the dogmas about Mary, that I forget about Mary herself. We should see and interact with Mary as she really is—our mother. That is, we should see Mary as a person and not as a dogma.

Years ago I re-entered the Church after several years fallen away. Not long after my re-entry to religion, I discovered a call-in radio show called Catholic Answers Live. One of the first memories I have of that radio show (which would eventually become a staple of my intellectual formation—it's not just a show but, by airwaves, a portable classroom) is one particular call regarding Mary. Apologist and convert Steve Ray was the guest. In his response to the caller's question, Steve pointed to St. Luke's Gospel and illustrated how Luke would have likely sat down face to face with Mary herself in order to know the details he so carefully recorded in his Gospel. (Note also that in his prologue he states his firm intention to write an "orderly account" of real events.) That statement—that Luke actually needed to hear Mary's voice in order to write what he wrote—was for me a profound realization that pointed toward the reality of the Gospels, and more importantly, the reality of the characters within the Gospels. The great thing about the Gospels as opposed to, say, *The Lord of the Rings*, is that the characters of the Gospels *live today*.

Imagine sitting face to face with Mary as Luke did. He records details about what Mary *felt* and *thought* during her encounter with the angel Gabriel. He also tells us that after the visit by the shepherds following Jesus' birth, Mary "pondered in her heart" what had occurred. How could Luke know about this unless he had been told firsthand? Indeed, Luke must have sat with Mary, looked into her eyes, and listened with keen concentration as her sweet voice retold the events as she could remember them. And certainly she would have recalled them with flawless vividness.

We know who Mary was for Luke, for his Gospel reveals profound insights into who he, along with the early Church, understood her to be. But again, who is Mary—right now—for you?

You can't love what you don't know; and each new thing you learn about someone is something new to love. Gaining knowledge is, therefore, key in the Christian life. But when gaining knowledge becomes an end in itself, and not a means that culminates in love, it becomes problematic. Again, Mary is a person, not a dogma. Marian dogmas describe Mary, but they are not *her*.

Allow me to digress for a moment. Doctrine is the Church's collective teachings on faith and morals. But, of course, there are different levels of Church teaching. Thus, dogmas are doctrines that have been infallibly defined by the Church. Dogmas are not created by the Church. They are everlasting truths that are revealed by God through the Church. All dogmas are doctrines, but not all doctrines are dogmas, since not all doctrines have reached that level of infallible certitude.

Stephen Hawking believes in the beginning of the universe; but he doesn't believe God did it. He doesn't believe anyone did it. He writes, "Because there is a law such as gravity, the universe can and will create itself from nothing." But only persons create. Laws don't *do* anything. They are descriptions and nothing more. Dogmas are much the same. This is why we must always love the person before the dogma.

God has told us much about Mary through the Church; hence, there are some things we can know dogmatically about her. She was born without original sin and full of grace, and was consequently preserved from all sin thereafter. She was also the Mother of Jesus, who was God always and everywhere—including of course while he was in Mary's womb—and thus she is rightfully called the Mother of God or *Theotokos* (God-bearer). These examples (there are more) of Marian dogmas, though communicated by the Church at different times through history, reflect the constant teaching of the Christian Church since the earliest centuries.

Mary is a person—as all the saints are. We believe, alongside twenty centuries of Christians, that the saints are given a special grace of interceding for us from before God's throne in heaven (see Rev. 5). The saints are the "great cloud of witnesses" (Heb. 12:1) who desire not to be merely spectators but to be personally involved in our lives as intercessors and friends. We will never sit at a banquet table with folks like Frodo or Peter Pan, but with friends like St. Joseph, Bl. Pier Giorgio Frassati, St. John Vianney, and Mary. The invitation has been issued and the table is set: this is a real opportunity and the price of admission is persevering love decorated with mercy unto our last breath. This is not fantasy; it is more real than the reality we know.

Mary, furthermore, takes a special place in our lives that even exceeds that of all the other saints: she is our intercessor, friend, and *mother*. This tradition of holding Mary to be the spiritual mother of the living—that is, of you and me—has its origin at the cross of Christ. "Behold your mother," said Jesus to John, who stood with Mary before their bloodied Savior (John 19:27). This has immediate consequences, for Jesus was about to die and did not have blood brothers of his own to care for his beloved mother; so he chose the "beloved disciple" to take in his mother and care for her. On death's door, every breath is precious and counted; our Lord labored to speak these words directly to John (and John was sure to record them). But the words "Behold your mother" spoken by Jesus to John were also spoken, on a deeper level, to all of humanity; and through the guidance of the Holy Spirit, the Church has maintained this (see 1 Tim. 3:15). There at the cross, Jesus gives his mother to St. John—and to us too—that we might also be under her protection and receive her guidance and help. The moment of adoption at the cross was climactic, as St. John's next verse testifies: "After this . . . Jesus knew that all was now finished" (John 19:28). St. Ambrose near the close of the fourth century wrote, "Our flesh was cast out of Paradise by a man and woman; it was joined to God through a Virgin. . . . Eve is called mother of the human race, but Mary Mother of salvation."

Just as we might call Eve our first mother "in the beginning," so also Mary might be seen as our everlasting mother from the new beginning onward. St. Irenaeus writes, "Just as Eve, having indeed a husband, Adam, but being nevertheless as yet a virgin . . . having become disobedient, was made the cause of death, both to herself and to the entire human race; so also did Mary, having a man betrothed [to her], and being nevertheless a virgin, by yielding obedience, became the cause of salvation, both to herself and to the entire human race. . . . And thus also it was that the knot of Eve's disobedience was loosed by the obedience of Mary."

Mary fulfills perfectly what Eve couldn't: God's will. And she untwists what Eve twisted. She is perfect inside and out—the true Ark of the Covenant. The original ark of the covenant is the holy container that held the stone tablets of the Ten Commandments, the miraculous manna of the Israelites, and the rod of Aaron that budded miraculously (Heb. 9:4). The ark was so holy that if one touched it he would die (see 2 Sam. 6:7). It was, in a sense, perfect: designed by God, made of imperishable acacia wood, and endowed inside and out with pure gold. It is no surprise therefore that Mary was eventually called the Ark of the New Covenant in the early Church.

Mary (in a clear parallel to the ark) held the Word of God (stone tablets), the Bread of Life (manna), and the High Priest (Aaron's staff). She was the sacred vessel who would be overshadowed by the Holy Spirit (Luke 1:35), just as the ark of the covenant would be overshadowed by the glory cloud of God (see Exod. 40:35). St. Luke also unveils Mary as the Ark of the New Covenant. With 2 Samuel 6 in mind, St. Luke describes what happens when Mary, newly pregnant, ventures to the home of her cousin Elizabeth, who is pregnant with John the Baptist. Elizabeth greets Mary, saying, "Blessed are you among women, and blessed is the fruit of your womb." On hearing Mary's voice, John "leaped" in his mother's womb (Luke 1:42, 44). We don't have to look to the Church Fathers to prove that the early Christians honored Mary with a profound reverence (but we certainly can!)—St. Luke's Gospel spells it out too.

Mary is a person, alive and glorified today. She is our mother, and will be for all of eternity. She loves you and me more than we could ever comprehend. As Frank Sheed has remarked, you can't love what you don't know. So get to know Mary even better! Read good books about her. Say the Rosary daily and really meditate on the mysteries. See the life of Christ through the eyes of Mary. And above all, speak with her and invite her intercession often through simple, little conversations—just as you do with your earthly mother. Mary is always listening and ready to act. As St. John Vianney has written, "Only after the Last Judgment will Mary get any rest; from now until then, she is much too busy with her children."

Art Index

.... † ....

The Joyful Mysteries

15   Orazio Gentileschi, *The Annunciation*, 1623, oil on canvas, 112.5 × 77.1 in., Galleria Sabauda, Turin, Italy, Wikimedia Commons, public domain.

19   Arthur Hacker, *The Annunciation*, 1892, oil on canvas, 91 × 49.5 in., Tate Britian, London, England, Wikimedia Commons, public domain.

23   José Moreno, *La Visitación*, 1662, oil on canvas, 72.8 × 51.9 in., Museo de Burgos, Burgos, Spain, Wikimedia Commons, public domain.

27   Fritz von Uhde, *Die Heilige Nacht (Triptychon)*, 1888, oil on canvas, 52.9 × 46 in., Staatliche Kunstsammlungen Dresden, Dresden, Germany, Wikimedia Commons, public domain.

31   Arent de Gelder, *Simeon's Song of Praise*, 1700, oil on canvas, 37.2 × 42.3 in., Royal Picture Gallery Mauritshuis, the Hague, Netherlands, Wikimedia Commons, public domain.

35   Circle of Jusepe de Ribera, *Jesus among the Doctors*, 1630, oil on canvas, 50.7 × 68.8 in., Kunsthistorisches Museum, Vienna, Austria, Wikimedia Commons, public domain.

The Sorrowful Mysteries

The Glorious Mysteries

The Luminous Mysteries

113 Peter Paul Rubens, *Last Supper*, 1631, oil on canvas, 119.6 × 98.4 in., Pinacoteca di Brera, Milan, Italy, Wikimedia Commons, public domain.